Feelings

Shy

Sarah Medina

Illustrated by Jo Brooker

Heinemann Library
Chicago, Illinois

© 2008 Heinemann Library
a division of Reed Elsevier Inc.
Chicago, Illinois

Customer Service 888–454–2279
Visit our website at www.heinemannlibrary.com

Photo research by Erica Martin
Designed by Jo Malivoire
Color Reproduction by Dot Gradations Ltd, UK
Printed in China by South China Printing Company Limited

12 11 10 09 08
10 9 8 7 6 5 4 3 2 1

Library of Congress Cataloging-in-Publication Data
Medina, Sarah, 1960-
  Shy / Sarah Medina; illustrated by Jo Brooker.
    p. cm. -- (Feelings)
  Includes bibliographical references and index.
  ISBN 978-1-4034-9795-6 (hc) -- ISBN 978-1-4034-9802-1 (pb)
  1. Bashfulness--Juvenile literature. I. Brooker, Jo, 1957- II.Title.
  BF575.B3M43 2007
  155.2'32--dc22
                        2007010550

Acknowledgments
The author and publisher are grateful to the following for permission to reproduce copyright material:
Bananastock p. 22A, D; Getty Images pp. 9 (Photodisc), 22 B (Taxi), 22 C (Taxi).

Every effort has been made to contact copyright holders of any material reproduced in this book. Any omissions will be rectified in subsequent printings if notice is given to the publisher.

Contents

Some words are shown in bold, **like this**. They are explained in the glossary on page 23.

What Is Shyness?

Shyness is a **feeling**. Feelings are something you feel inside. Everyone has different feelings all the time.

happy

sad

shy

4

When you feel shy, you may find it
hard to talk to people you do not
know well.

What Happens When I Feel Shy?

When you are shy, you may feel
as if you want to hide.

If you are shy, you might feel hot and shaky inside when someone talks to you. You may **blush** and find it hard to talk.

Why Do I Feel Shy?

You may feel shy when you meet
new children.

You may feel shy when you have to do something in front of people.

Is It Okay to Feel Shy?

Lots of people feel shy sometimes.
There is nothing wrong with being shy.

You can try to become less shy. You can invite new friends to play with you.

What Can I Do If I Feel Shy?

If you feel shy, tell someone who cares about you. Talking about your **feelings** helps them pass.

Try joining in, even if you feel shy. It could be fun! You will feel less shy when you know people better.

Will I Always Feel Shy?

You may feel shy now, but **feelings** change all the time.

You might feel more shy sometimes and less shy at other times. Remember, this is normal—and it is okay!

How Can I Tell If Someone Feels Shy?

When people feel shy, they may be very quiet. They may not want to join in if you are playing.

Some people may be too shy to look at you. Remember, they are not being rude. They are just shy.

Can I Help When Someone Feels Shy?

You can help people who are shy. Be kind and tell them that you really want to play with them.

Ask them if they are okay. Tell them that you will help them until they feel better.

I Feel Better Now!

Remember, everyone feels shy
sometimes. Shyness does not
last forever.

It is good to learn what to do about shyness. Then you can help yourself and other people, too!

What Are
These Feelings?

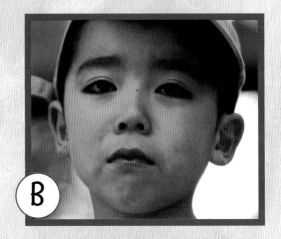

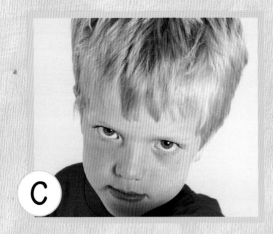

Which of these people look happy?
What are the other people feeling?
Look at page 24 to see the answers.

Picture Glossary

blush

when your face or neck
turns pink or red and
feels hot

feeling

something that you feel
inside. Shyness is a feeling.

Index

Answers to the questions on page 22

The person in picture A looks happy. The other people could be sad, shy, or angry.

Note to Parents and Teachers

Reading for information is an important part of a child's literacy development. Learning begins with a question about something. Help children think of themselves as investigators and researchers by encouraging their questions about the world around them. Most chapters in this book begin with a question. Read the question together. Look at the pictures. Talk about what you think the answer might be. Then read the text to find out if your predictions were correct. Think of other questions you could ask about the topic, and discuss where you might find the answers. Assist children in using the picture glossary and the index to practice new vocabulary and research skills.